Night Work

Night Work

POEMS

C. E. Perry

Sarabande Books
LOUISVILLE, KENTUCKY

FIRST EDITION

Managing Editor
Sarabande Books, Inc.
2234 Dundee Road, Suite 200
Louisville, KY 40205

Library of Congress Cataloging-in-Publication Data

Perry, C. E. (Carole Elizabeth), 1968–
   Night work : poems / by C.E. Perry. — 1st ed.
      p.   cm.
   Includes bibliographical references.
   ISBN 978-1-932511-67-3 (pbk. : acid-free paper)
   I. Title.
   PS3616.E7928N54 2009
   811'.6—dc22   2008009817

ISBN-13: 978-1-932511-67-3

Cover image: *Angel of Waking Dreams* by Beverley Ashe, provided courtesy of the artist.

Cover and text design by Charles Casey Martin

Manufactured in Canada
This book is printed on acid-free paper.

Sarabande Books is a nonprofit literary organization.

The Kentucky Arts Council, a state agency in the Commerce Cabinet, provides operational support funding for Sarabande Books with state tax dollars and federal funding from the National Endowment for the Arts, which believes that a great nation deserves great art.

C O N T E N T S

Night Work

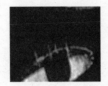

No Flashlight

It is too cold for August. The moon, one
hoof-print deep, hardens over the lake.

Around my ankles, minnows hide and seek —
delicate fin-fan. I should go back to the house.

I should pull the windows down to their
devout, polished-pine frames and say

nothing of the night leaning on the lake's
surface, nothing of a pin loosening,

nothing of that clear-eyed cavalry
shifting its weight in the summer grass.

Anatomy

My lungs are two dogs
stumbling off of the track.
Your shoulders are boys
leaning back on their luck.

My head is a girl
lifted up by a bell.
Your tongue is a seal
slipping under a swell.

My arms are the aunts
swimming back to the dock.
Your eyes are a swamp
of tripwire and shock.

My knees are egg cups
buried deep in the dirt.
Your hips are the tips
of chopsticks that hurt.

My hands are the cooks
who simmer and poach.
Your hands are the cooks
who stay late and smoke.

My mouth is a box
where your name used to be.
Your heart is a watch
unfastened by me.

Acknowledgments

The baby pulls itself around the mother's breast,
a curving need. Light comes to the mother's face.
It is the countermelody. The angled prow of her

arm, her unified movement, her yes—this painter
obeys the laws of gentleness, of coping. She knows
how the human body is broken down into a trellis

of lines. She knows, for instance, how one's mouth
will be drawn shut after the funeral. She knows
how one's abortion is a three-dimensional procedure

of scratched lines around the soft red pip.
When emptiness enters a painting, there is depth.
The eye needs time to dissolve. For these

figures to stand out against the background,
she creates a series of interruptions. With shape
and hue, one must always risk losing control.

Thank you for the unexpected breaks and mistakes
that helped this woman paint. Thank you for
the fever, the drizzle, the standing still. Thank you

for the incomplete heart that knows no valid
boundary. Thank you for luck's endless changing
of position and for the oblique progress of failure.

Thank you for two legs walking, for the distance
between branches, for the vertical, for the horizontal,
for the confusion, for the vista, for the wall.

Thank you for the violent red center of memory,
for the thin economy of the painter's wrist,
and for the baby's mouth, opening.

In Indiana

Dead hogs swing in the barn —
discordant pendulums

holding the hour. She braces
each sheep with her thighs

and the wool spills over
like foaming beer. It is

just necessary, nothing
exotic. While the doves

sleep, her pelvis and arms
force time across one

deliberate axis, leaving
the sheep to shiver in

their new blue skin.
This is how the past

becomes the past. This
is how work gets done.

When I Was Eight

One April evening, I just kept going.
I ran through all the lawns and sprinklers,
through cornfields, past any place where

things were planted. I ran through an
empty zoo, past the parade, past the
mighty Roman Empire. I ran past

Queen Isabel of Spain in her yellow gown,
through the tennis ball factory, past roads
I would never choose, and past choice itself.

I ran past debt and war and the waiting
room, past Eleanor Roosevelt in her itchy
wool coat, past the dumpster and the body

inside it. I ran past my husband, past my
wife, and past three children building
a careful bridge. I ran past a giant silk

fan, taut as an insect's wing, unfolding
teal and silver in the evening light. When
I got to the end, the air was cold, like snow.

I caught my breath and watched the fan
tilt from a huge and gentle hand. Then I
pulled up my socks and walked home.

Peaches

His truck pulls up too fast and when
he shuts the door, a purpose slows
his eyes. The air wilts and the fence
leans away while water drips from a

sleeping hose. The boy rides in on his
bike, fruit in the bag. While the woman
chews on her trapped leg, the dog races
the length of its life, loose in the heat.

The woman looks alone in the world—
as if she were already dead. When the
man's fist knocks her down, the peaches
wait on the stairs, but the boy is nowhere.

Summer Horses

When the sun nails itself to the field
and the barn kneels in the heat,

what else could we do but leave saddles
unlifted and take our mares to the river?

We ride bareback down dirt roads single file.
We don't weigh much. It is July 1975;

our bodies have not yet suffered
and our minds are still neatly folded.

Rumps drip sweat as they take their
measured steps. The horses stop to drink

but we urge them deeper, so they stumble
in, giving ragged moans when the water

takes their weight. We glide, cold river
swift at our hips—life bright in loose

time, under formal tall trees,
three girls given and received.

The Circus Girl's Remarkable Suspension

The rope unwinds, her sequined torso spins —
a leashed torpedo. Her legs split the air;
wide calipers can measure any sin.

Her fingers touch what feels like warm chagrin
as poodles crash toy cars without a care.
The rope unwinds, her sequined torso spins.

Tears of the poorly trained bear converge
in the ringmaster's eyes: trapped history shared.
Wide calipers can measure any sin.

What kind of night would let itself begin
with such abandon, sloppy with despair?
The rope unwinds, her sequined torso spins.

The audience identifies her skin
as its own, a turbid mix of cells spared.
Wide calipers can measure any sin.

In this moment, held by one aching pin,
our lives undo beyond what we would dare.
Our rope unwinds, her sequined torso spins;
wide calipers can't measure all our sins.

Miss Chanel Invents the Little Black Dress

Her friends waltzed from the orphanage
down the dirt road toward town.
She saw them try

and she saw them fail —
inventing princes and parties,
holding their perfect arms wide

for no one. Gabrielle
hitched a ride on the ice wagon
to the race track, and took her

usual seat, next to everyone.
They were all here: men who
had grunting sex in alleys,

the women who let them,
bankers with bow ties, newly-
hatched shop girls, the Duchess

and her fine-boned lover in smart hats.
Six horses pounded the earth round,
making a place for themselves

in the fat French heat. Gentlemen
licked sweat from their lips. Dark
horses circled under the water spout.

Money rested quiet and tabulated
in a vault at the center of France, and
the Duchess, knowing this, unbuttoned

her lover's white lace collar, and touched
her neck where her pulse galloped.
The girl's face was as placid as a toy soldier's,

but her body dropped slowly to
one knee, like a camel bowing to the
moon while sands rise into storms.

Chief Complaint

I took this flu medicine because my
friend gave it to me when I saw dead parrots
in her tub and then I got this rash on
my back that feels like somebody scrubbed it
with bloodwater and stars and I don't have
a fever but my eyes hurt when I laugh
which I don't do very often because
my Raymond drinks and hits me but he has
a tough job and his boss is mean and has
a head like a shark except with yellow hair and
he wants to have another baby but
I want to get this snake out of my head
and sleep through the night and stop seeing ghosts
on the patio who hiss at me and
say things about my soul and how much ice cream
I eat because my throat hurts with this flu.

We Can't

He swears at each meeting of the clean
that he, too, has sweated every stupor,
has yanked his craving like so many teeth
from every nerve and neurotransmitter.
But his need stares him down from the back seat.
He stops in the Safeway parking lot, makes a little
lean-to from morphine and some skin pulled neat.
His blind lynx paws from tree to tree, each brittle
branch fracturing as he springs for his life —
the last living thing in a desolate land.
Our brown-eyed boy, narcotics for a wife,
pours himself away with such a steady hand.
We change the locks, we weep, we watch him go.
We want to know how far he'll fall, but no —

Ode To Reverend Bumperton

Praise to the pie-faced warrior, with
his simultaneous eyes and polio leg!
Praise to the life force that travels
through his hair and generates a Field of
Generous Multiplicity around him.
Stand close to the Reverend Bumperton!
Note his Polish arms, his Spanish thighs.
His hidden reality is as fierce as an
egg chugging along the pink horizon.
Kiss the Reverend Bumperton! Grasp
his raincoat and smell the naked wires
in his breath. Step into the primary flower!
Who cares what the choirmaster will say?

God's Peculiar Care

Mama, I have escaped from
the Institute of Defectology.
The spooky castles, the dazed blue dogs,
the lithium salt-licks are all behind me now.

I detangled the cellar walls.
I licked my cup.

I had a special technique of never
lifting myself more than
seventeen degrees above the ambient
condensation of despair. Oh yes,

materials were provided: newspaper,
needles, nightgowns,
sweat, loneliness
and coffee. Sometimes

there was coffee. We sat among the happy
clocks, the stuffed cloth dolls, the tinfoil
altar to our tarred and feathered God,
gulping coffee that Janine had made
on the sly. She was the only nurse

who said our names. It has taken me
seven years to pull out the
hook and another two

to get round and round myself in
permanent black.
I have chewed a wad of irreverence
from the nut house floor.

Open my clean and peaceful casket,
if you must.
I've paid my clay nanny to lie there
and I've paid her very well.

Whatever I can carry. Whatever
I can run with.
Tonight I sew bits of myself
by hand to the core.

Sunday at the Boat Building School

When a garden of amputees feels
the rudderless shadow of a seagull,

the accelerated permission
of the bird wakes up

loose and right and disobedient,
dipping into the uneven light

where our besotted wasp, not
ours at all, chews wet wood.

Song for Her

sop churn fiddle spoon
      catch your baby in the net
tilting stem bitter thread
      did you catch that baby yet
skinny soot tinder star
      do you stand on solid ground
thirsty loft nimble thud
      can the river pull you round
tight blue whimsy glass
      feel the roots dig through your sight
peachy ache pepper thought
      while six minutes hang the night
wilted source creamy sob
      that life you had is reaching back
rotten sauce thimble spell
      but cannot find you in the black
quaking pearl sugar girl
      what you want is rare and gone
muddy sick petal palm
      someone here will see you home

Lachrymosa

Wisteria curls around the church door
like smoke with small green bones. There is no hand

to hold. Mourners remove their raincoats and
hang them on the rack beside St. Francis

and the lamb. She has been dead for three days.
It is time to let go of the girl who

planted the wild vine, who pounded and yelled,
who dismantled herself and lowered the

moon by spoonfuls into a puddled grave.
She was a starlet's hip, a sidecar breeze,

. a map of the world. It feels like spring this
morning. The magnolia is wide open.

We will miss her and miss her and miss her.

Dora's Devotee

Dora's building a rocket
and she makes me watch her
do it. She makes me lie

about our plans and methods.
She calls me the Associate.
I know I'm sidekick to a flawed

and doomed hero. She twists
a branch like her father bends her
arm. Then we dismember

stolen appliances looking for
deflection coils, ejector buttons. She says
we'll probably have to go up

one at a time. That night
I sleep on the ceiling—my cheek
hot, pressed against her back.

Our rocket coughs past the bald, lonely
planets. A short note is pinned to her coat:
I am Dora. I will not die tonight.

The Vivian Sisters in the Realms of the Unreal

One is for our phosphorous temple that crumbled in the storm.
The monkeys warned of a darkness coming.

Two is for the nations regarded by God —
trading spices for children — salt and cumin
shoveled into strange boats, Girl-girls and Girl-boys
climbing the thorn trees, weeping.

Three is for the awesome density of our existence:
a thimbleful weighs thirty-six billion tons.

Four is for the Worker, the Talker, the Nude,
and the Miraculous Shepherd who unfailingly
persist on our behalf.

Five is for the stages of the cooling of the stars:
the Heat Puffing Stage, the Stage of Velvet Softening,
the Carbon Inter-Conversion, the Stage of Regret,
and the White Giant Stage. Praise to every star,
every stuttering furnace!

Six is for the six kinds of air we have created:
Common Air, Vital Air, Pure Air, Disciplined Air,
Fierce Air, and Air Between All Things.

Seven is for us, the Seven Morally Perfect Vivian
Sisters. We shall lead the Child-Slave Rebellion for
we are the vortex of human capacity!

Eight is for the Fantastic Elsewhere.

Nine is for the Nine Energized Proofs of Intent
which explain the Tainting of Liquids, the Geometrical
Strata of Reliance, and the Belonging of Everything.

Ten is for the ten-chambered heart of the Long Bird
who flies over us with kindness and sadness and care.

Lucky

Of course I have changed since I last saw you.
That was ten years ago, when I still told time
and drank my coffee black. I sweeten it up now.

I don't argue much. I don't lock the doors. When
wild horses visit in the night and eat my garden,
I let them. They're just hungry and have lost

their way. I sit, admiring how they gnaw through rows
of lush basil, sweet tomatoes, tender squash blossoms,
innocently putting an end to the whole damn thing.

Bad Rice

My friend's husband was once sitting in a bar
with his old college buddies, talking about how

the past twenty-five years had given them
wonderful families and well-paying jobs. Then

the most successful of them left the bar
and was run over by an ice-cream truck.

Another friend was biking down his street
thinking how perfectly his life was unfolding

when a car door tossed him, breaking his arms.
Though one may feel content, or even happy,

perhaps it is unwise to say it out loud. If you
win the lottery, it's probably best just to

nod your head and finish washing the dishes,
lest you be struck with meningitis. As you walk

on the beach with your lover and your heart
swells with grace, perhaps it is best only to say,

"this is not entirely unpleasant," lest the aneurysm
in your brain rupture like a tiny volcano. As you

gaze on the sleeping faces of your healthy children,
remember the Japanese farmer who scatters the seeds

that will save him from misery and starvation,
blessing each handful, saying: "Bad rice, bad rice."

After Someone Dies

It has been a month, or maybe more since
they sent the orchid. See, it has small spots
of teal at the part where petals convince
each other to reach belly-up, around and out
like a witch's shoe when the witch is snuffed.
We've had so many flowers here, all gone
now. Only the orchid with its velvety ruff
survived the emptiness. It is the one
living thing we all can bear to see—the snooze
of its alien head nodding at the wreck
we've almost become. Dear So and So, thank you
for sending us this useless visitor. Its effect
is chilling and calming and politely insane;
we no longer expect to outlast our pain.

How To Build a Box

All things shrink and expand.
All wood, being made of atoms

and bits of the indecipherable void, forgives
to some extent. No mistake will undo

you. Each box requires a maker.
Gentle builder, bring the full strength

of your humanity to these choices. Rosewood with
blind hinges? Hickory with a book-matched

two-piece lid? Ash covered with a devilish
weave of rose petals and wasp stings?

Consider the spectrum of dynamic tension,
how things fit and resist: wood to nail,

nail to hammer, hammer to hand, hand
to eye, eye to hawk, hawk to God, God

to worm, and worm to wood. Are you
essentially a thief? A nuisance? A gathering

of untended energies? Hopeful builder,
fit the corners flush and tight, lip to lid.

The box will sit on your mantle in the moonlight,
a monument of careful proportions, a true

humdinger. Then you will open it
and hear what you've been trying to say.

On Waking

Snow falls from those tall branches,
sinking like shipwreck,
making the same
measureless sound.
All of it comes down.
We grow ripe and strange
in my velvet eye
as raw time prisms,
slurs,
then regenerates at your skin's
bright edge.

Bonita and the Bird Doctor

He rolls up his sleeves, bows once
to Suffering, and once to Relief,
then unfastens a square leather case

containing instruments for wing repair,
a small glass syringe, and three vials
of original vaccines for fever, ennui,

and clouded, demented flight.
He reapproximates the wing.
Ninety-three million miles away,

the sun distributes amber light over
the Bird Doctor and his good patient.
They are luminous this afternoon.

Oh, how the frequency swells, enriching
every particle, every wave of being!
Each one listens for the others:

the polished mahogany table,
the swallow's blinking eye, this
tension on the tiny string, and his

own pulse, institutional and fierce —
like a clock in a locked museum.
Tomorrow he will be transformed

by telling Bonita why he became
the Bird Doctor. She will hold
his shy chin, widen the angles of

his attention, and understand him.
But today they have not yet met.
She is swimming in the lake,

displacing the water with her
fabulous arms, feeling the sun
shine through her like an atomic bomb.

Of Patterns and Purpose

Tonight, I lift the curtain and watch
that white rose bowing to the sea
then to me like an old butler.

We are tucked in at the edges
for now, for now. The crack
in this porcelain bowl proves

that the order of things can be
rearranged by delicate forces.
We are a thin vein of the ponderous

whole. My ordinary face in the moonlight,
this chipped blue bowl, the commonness
of common objects: this rose rests

equally in the wind and that rock's
inhospitable surface. I need you
truly and exactly. By pure

chance I know this
when the waves break open
a crazed green hum.

Past Curfew

Evangeline, the way you dance makes
marks on me, makes my hawks jump

up and smile. That skirt hugs you
like a sleepy kid and I want your

percolating heart to articulate.
I'm just the drummer, another

beer and bow tie, midnight sweat
storming. But thou and thine

is racing me and mine. Man, your
hips go bump to Peru, no suitcase.

Why Lovers in Trouble End Up at the Rodeo

We have driven eighty-seven miles and paid
four dollars each to see that cowboy's wrist
snap like fresh chalk. My love, the meadows
are pressed flat by the young Montana backs
of young Montana men. It stuns us to witness
such torque and to crave it. It stuns us to recall
bookshelves fainting to the floor and rats
swimming away from us in bed. We are still
alive and the beer is cold. We each swoon
when our hero takes flight—his hat a swank
hurrah, his head lost, loose over those horns.

Fairy Tales

This bed is not a boat. There is no sea.
When our baby girl falls off the edge, she

lands on all fours and screams out for us, for
the light and the hands and the holding. Lift

her above your heart, her perfect head, neck
supple as a porpoise, busy little

heart pluck pluck plucking: happy red banjo.
Our yard is rooted to bedrock by a

thirsty oak; its subterranean sip
thrums through our sleep, buds unfurling, flexing—

the endless north and south of sap. Listen
to green praying in the temple of green,

to our white sheets untucking, to the witch
gliding up the moonlit stairs.

Supplicant

Give the doe that extra
glance of the road, a safer
path through the ice.

Give me back your face,
tearless and illuminated
as it was that January night

in my car. Give us our lives
before we learned that sedimentary
rock is formed from hair

and fur: fragments pulled
from their homes, then
deposited elsewhere forever.

Prospero's Correlative

From my side of the bed, I see across our street,
that neighbor holding his baby girl in orbit on
the second-floor porch. Legs giggle around his grasp
as he offers her uncivilized body—aviatrix
absolutely small. Eclipsing the porch light, her head
could be Jupiter and I hear moths twitching in Honduras,
contributing to the last of twelve billion breaths
that put a hurricane in business. Caliban builds me
his first fire, fingernails deep with dirt. Neptune's
methane and nitrogen spark rich geysers into
constant storms. Resting the structure of my cheek
against your shoulder, I feel longitude cross latitude.
Will we love the velocity of ships if the anchors
don't work? If sand, like sugar, proves too fine?

Limitations of Photography

She holds the broken
baby, tracing his face.

She will use the picture to
remember how he got smaller

and smaller until he was
a spoonful of buttery light

and then gone. She thinks
she will never stand,

never sleep. Memorizing him,
she does not look up.

She does not see herself
concerned with other children,

too busy mothering to recall
when the mother was first born.

I Need Eggs

I need matches and figs and peace.
I need berries and words and money.
Of course, money. I need eggs and

sugar and coffee. I need a room full
of epiphytic orchids that live on
nothing but fog. I need a view.

I need my friend Gerry to step
out with me, cut a rug. I need
some Windex to take the scum

off things. I need a consistent
backward dive. I need more thread.
I need those little Chinese paper

lanterns with real silk tassels.
I need an ambassador. I need
a more compassionate mind

and children and cinnamon-
flavored toothpicks all in one
bag so I can carry them home.

Learning About Water

The moon, once million-eyed and chuckling,
goes blind as a plate. Elsewhere other hands
take to sleep as if it were the wider hand
and I am all the dog, sniffing out back for
unmentionables. One night, we left our
skin sleeping in camp, and elfed to the river.
I remember the grip in your laugh, your
tight stance in the crosscurrents. Now
I look for missing things. I see you send
fistfuls of pennies spinning to high ceilings.
I watch smoke and winter, wait for you to pass.
I wish us safe into blackberries and the blue
of storybook forests. Even then you knew.
The crafty can be juiced by the craftier.
In the fragile berserk of dying, did you feel
how the river spilled wild from our wrists?

Sullivan's Island, South Carolina

I see the palmetto leaves from my chair on
the porch—they twist back, showing how hard
an ocean breeze can grab. The neighbors laugh,

painting white trim on their rusted garage.
The worn flag snaps to on its bright pole.
This is not my house. Someone has placed

roses on the table next to me. Four o'clock
heat unhinges a petal and gives it to
the floor. I've been out here almost all day.

I wish I could feel this tin ache relenting. If only
the worst were over. My breath lifts the petal
a little as a pillaging tide spins and spills.

October

All the summer babies
can hold their heads up now,

each neck a fresh stalk of
white asparagus. Their

plummy hearts churn beneath
powdered skin, while green leaves

turn voraciously gold,
fainting to the sidewalk

under their strollers. The
sheets have been washed again

and again, made soft, fierce
and ready for winter.

My Mother the Teacher Talks about War

When kids learn things they are put in rows.
The good kids, the ones with clean socks,
whose parents read Dr. Seuss and make animal-
shaped pancakes on Saturday mornings,

those kids sit in the back because they can work
without much help. Then there are the other kids—
the ones with uncombed hair, and stomachs
full of Cheez Whiz who have no bedtime,

no winter coats. These are the kids who sit
up front so the teacher can keep them in line.
They are the ones who fight our battles for us.
They think they have no choice but to run

into crossfire, storm the beach, secure the city.
They patrol the wall in the uniforms they have
been given. They built the wall because someone
told them to. And, when ordered, they will destroy it.

Carousel, Central Park

Round and round on winter's frozen foot
ponies lift and sink, bright and brown, brains
cold as a handful of lake water.

The clop clop of the police horse trot
fits the tune wheezing through the ancient
German speakers. Trees stand like tent poles,

holding the heavy November sky.
It is about to snow. Bless our girl
in the worn blue parka who grabs the

brass pole with one hand and reaches her
other hand out to the air. Bless the
tangle that is her hair, her grin, her

ten-year-old self riding the wide-eyed
pony. She is filled with the primary
push. She thrusts into life like

the Himalayas, like a weed, like
the coiled filament in a glass bulb.
I have seen her on a real horse, bangs

damp, working her uncertainty loose,
dislodging it with a slow canter,
outrunning it for a stride or two.

I have seen her chewing the smallest
mistake to pulp, then crumple like a
shot deer. To her, feelings are Persian—

compelling, incomprehensible.
She looks at a field of daffodils
and sees an army of yellow cups,

not growth, not warmth, not the grace of spring.
How will she find her way? How will she
know on whose shoulder to lay her head?

When the music stops, when she steps down
from her still horse, the world will not be
flat. It will be unraveling. When

she looks for us, we will be there—our
uneven arms reaching for her, our
imperfect hearts, hives of royal love.

Make us all into a simpler shape:
a sphere of infinite radius
its center, this carousel, turning,

our girl rising up as the snow falls,
as the ponies slow, dense with purpose,
and the police horse circles the park.

Liturgy

Ash collects on the high bricks
where no one can see. Mother

stirs her drink with a mother's
touch. What holds this room

as still as a mixing bowl?
It will not, will not confess.

If only a bone would appear
on the plush carpet—evidence

at the feet of Abraham, his well-
chosen wife, and his delicious

daughter for whom he has
given thanks and praise.

Want and Fuss

I've seen a mountain slip, suddenly
divided. I know how done feels.
Done is the blotting of lips before

sauce, saxophones, a kiss-off; it's
luck unhooking as if by wise hands.
Done is the day, the cut, the blush,

the piped sighs of eighteen-wheelers —
not this praying mantis prowling exact
loops at your mouth, wary and shut.

Radiology

What is alive in you is everything:
bud and curl, contoured rivers, continents
and the shifting faults between them, our map

on the table, your tears on the map. My
compass needle spins in you. Gravity
lives in you. So does hope, emulsified —

gluing cell to cell. When you breathe, you are
the best berry of the sun-drunk berries,
a diamond humming in the quiet mine.

When you write, words fly to your brain like darts
to a bull's eye, and a magnificent
sea lumbers and froths where, moments before,

there were only bones and sand. When you sleep,
what is alive in you lies down too, but
does not rest, never no not ever stops

pulling good breath from nowhere. When you cry,
tears from the original reservoir
mix with saffron, opium, and the dew

falling from the tall, sad tree inside you.
I've touched this tree. Silently I finger
the roots. We have so much to surrender.

Wind with Tree

On the east wall of the Charleston gallery,
a tree stands alone in the lower corner

of the fifty-four-inch canvas. It is disarmingly
small, like a dollhouse door on a real house.

The rest of the painting is consumed by a
delicately curving tornado which is

gray as a rotten tooth, thin as the lips of disaster.
It swells around the origin of pain —

that formal center where there is no breath,
no pilot, no grace. The tree is as still as I am,

caught in the resin of final understanding.
Outside, a gush of Dixieland jazz falls into

tune. We lurch shamelessly — the tree, the topspin
screaming wind, the painter crying in his sleep,

my sweaty face turning away as if slapped.
The guests begin to dance, couples swing —

pulling each other to an unsteady center,
arriving and resisting with equal pleasure.

Night Work

Again, I find myself in the car
choosing the same bizarre route
past the Chinese restaurant that

is not there, then into the fairgrounds
I've never seen. I scrutinize each child
as they spin, pie-eyed and laughing but

cannot find you. I try to get help
but the police station is dark and
the lot is empty. As I do every night,

I unpack the car in case you somehow
got wedged without my knowing.
I shovel out all that salt, piles of it,

leaving that woozy eel to flip and toss
on the asphalt. Finally, I remember.
I walk to the hospital like a broken bone,

up the corridor that smells of warm blankets
and into the nursery where all the young
pretty nurses weep and dig at their eyes.

Your body is too cold, so I put you back under
my ribs where you belong, but every morning
you're gone and I am pithed, kissed, and alive.

ACKNOWLEDGMENTS

Grateful acknowledgment is made to the editors of the following journals in which these poems first appeared, often in different versions: *Alchemy, Dogwood, Little Patuxent Review, New South, Pool, Southeast Review,* and *The Southern Review*.

I am deeply grateful to Sarah Gorham and the Sarabande crew.

I thank all of my teachers, especially Julie Bruck, Gerald Stern, and Pat Skarda.

I thank Sally and Chuck Greer for providing sanctuary when I most needed it. I thank the Elizabeths (Brixius, Dessouky, Posner, and Stuckey-French) for their sturdy friendship. I am grateful to my mother.

Rita Mae and Charlotte are my inspiration every day.

NOTES FOR SELECTED POEMS

1. "God's Peculiar Care" was inspired by the life of Frances Farmer.
2. "Bad Rice" was inspired by the stories Elizabeth Stuckey-French told to me.
3. "Lachrymosa" is for Laurie Williams.
4. "The Vivian Sisters in the Realms of the Unreal" was inspired by the art of Henry Darger.
5. "Radiology" is for Rita Mae.
6. "Wind with Tree" is for Sally Greer, who took me to the Charleston art gallery.
7. "Night Work" is for my son, Charlie, who was with me from May 3 to May 8, 2004.

THE AUTHOR

C. E. Perry was born in Atlanta, Georgia. She graduated from the Iowa Writers' Workshop and from Dartmouth Medical School. Her poems have appeared in *The Southern Review, Southeast Review, Alchemy,* and *Pool.* She is a family medicine physician at a community health clinic in San Francisco where she lives with her family.

Shelley Eades

ᢒᢦ for Rita Mae ᢒᢦ